CONSCIOUSLY HEALING MS

It's Simple, But Not Easy

SHANNON HAKE

Copyright © 2024 by Shannon Hake

All rights reserved. No part of this book may be used or reproduced in any form whatsoever without written permission and proper citation. No part of this book was written with AI.

For more information, contact the following:

Heal.MS@yahoo.com
http://www.shannonhake.com/heal

The author's intent is only to offer information of a general nature to help you in your quest for emotional and spiritual well-being. If you use any of the information in this book for yourself, which is your constitutional right, the author assumes no responsibility for your actions.

Cover design by Zoey Aman

For anyone who has struggled with MS.

I understand and know this struggle firsthand. There are real reasons why you have MS and real answers for healing it.

If you are reading this book and willing to put in the effort, know you can heal.
My greatest wish is that you take this information, apply it wholeheartedly, and heal yourself.

CONTENTS

	Gratitude	vi
1	My MS Diagnosis Story	1
2	Real Answers	3
3	A Virus?	5
4	Where I Started	9
5	Simple, Not Easy	11
6	Know Your Why	15
7	Know Better, Do Better	19
8	How Do You Heal?	21
	This is How I've Been Healing My MS	22
9	Other Symptoms Healed	27
	FAQ	29
	Tips	33
	About the Author	35
	References, Sources, Citations	37

According to Oxford Languages:

To **heal** is to cause a wound, injury, or person to become sound or healthy again.

To **cure** is to relieve a person or animal of the symptoms of a disease or condition.

GRATITUDE

I thank Anthony William, The Medical Medium, for sharing information so freely with the world about how to heal hundreds of conditions and symptoms—information in every book you have written. I am incredibly, deeply grateful.

I thank Spirit of Compassion (SOC) for giving correct, life-saving information to Anthony William (AW). I thank AW for dedicating his life to passing on this information. I thank you both for helping those like me who are chronically ill find answers to their illness and how to heal.

I thank my daughter, Ayanna, for making food I will eat. It has been a salve for my tender wounds. I thank my husband, Dave, for his financial support. Without it, I would not have been able to follow the protocols in all the books and heal.

I thank Nicolette Bischof, Donna Darby, Deb Stone, Deb Yeats, Liz Manes-Ruhl, Suresh Rao, Dee Sullivan, Mark Lauterbach, Joseph Flanigan, Julie Keith, Jess Tankerlsey, Margaret and Wiff Withey, Ann Scott, Carolyn and Richard Ansted, and Molly Zraik for moral and emotional support.

I thank everyone who believed in me; you know who you are, and I am deeply grateful for your kindness. I also thank all the people who did not believe in me. I have grown because of you.

CHAPTER 1

MY MS DIAGNOSIS

December 26, 1999, was the day my life changed. I was 31 years old. I woke up, and half my body was numb. It was as if someone had sliced me down the middle from head to toe. I thought I had suffered a stroke. I kept tripping over things, stumbling over words, choking on water, and having trouble swallowing food. I was scared. I was a divorced, single mom of three young children. I didn't have room in my life to be sick.

All I could think was, "What am I going to do? How will I work and take care of my children?" So, I did what most people without medical insurance do: I waited to see if the symptoms would subside. After three weeks, the symptoms did subside and slowly improved.

Before the onslaught of my symptoms, I had enrolled in a nine-month IT program and started classes two weeks later. Six months into the program, the other half of my body became numb. Once again, my thinking slowed, I choked on water, and my emotions were heightened and unpredictable. What was going on? I was scared, panicky scared. How would I finish school and get a job if I couldn't think clearly?

I graduated in November with a Certificate in Applied Information Technology and was so excited and proud of myself; however, I knew something was very wrong with my body. I couldn't think straight or remember things. I slurred my speech, tripped over my own feet and was losing my eyesight in one eye. I was terrified!

I went to see my healer friend, and she would make the symptoms disappear. Within a week, they would come back, and she would help me again. After several sessions, she lovingly told me something was happening, and she couldn't help. I needed to see a medical doctor.

I went to a doctor, and she ordered an MRI. They found "MS-like" lesions in my brain, and she sent me to a Neurologist. The Neurologist gave me a stack of information on MS. This included information about administering a "disease-modifying" injection once a week, Avonex.

After a year and a half, I couldn't do it anymore. The flu-like side effects were not worth it, and the actual act was too much for me to commit week after week.

Five different medications and 14 years later, I finally said, enough is enough! I am not doing this for the rest of my life. I decided my diet was my medicine; The food I put in my body would heal me.

I had no idea how true that statement would turn out to be for me.

"Your body does not attack itself. Pathogens do."

-Shannon Hake

CHAPTER 2

REAL ANSWERS

Neurologists told me they don't know the cause and don't have a cure. They also said to me that my body was confused and was attacking itself. I believed them, of course, because they are doctors, and they should know. But they didn't know, and it was only a theory from the 1950s. It's not their fault; it's what they were taught in medical school.

    Fourteen years after diagnosis, my body was noticeably going downhill. One morning when I awakened, I had another new symptom, constant dizziness. Walking, showering, cooking, driving, reading, and most things were challenging. Over the next five years, I visited my acupuncturist, neurologist, physical therapist, healer, anyone I could think of, but nothing helped. My husband had to take over the cooking, shopping, and cleaning. I used a cane and walker for stability. I spent more time indoors, unable to do things outside without my walker or cane. My symptoms became worse, with no end in sight. This was especially true about my bladder. I couldn't go on fun hikes with my friends or take walks with my husband anymore. Whenever I went out with a group, I would make everyone wait while I found a restroom. I felt like a burden, and it was easier for everyone if I didn't go.

    At this point, I was desperate for any relief and a sense of normalcy in my life. I looked online for anything that might help me. I tried the keto diet, paleo diet, diatomaceous earth, bentonite clay, apple cider vinegar, high-dose vitamin D, daily B2, and fish oil. None of them helped my lengthy list of symptoms; To reiterate, I had optic neuritis, constant numbness with tingling in my hands and feet. I was choking on water, tripping over nothing, had muscle spasms in my legs, slurred my speech, had migraines, dizziness, fatigue, brain fog[61], sensitivity to heat and cold, trouble putting thoughts together, difficulty staying asleep and awake, bladder and bowel issues, and 'sandbags' in my legs. I was unable to hold a singing tune anymore. I knew deep down that my body was not doing this to itself. However, I didn't know what was causing this.

It was about this time when a friend stopped by and gave me a book by Anthony William, *Medical Medium, Secrets Behind Chronic and Mystery Illness and How to Finally Heal*[1]. I was intrigued by the title and even more intrigued by the contents inside. When I read the part revealing that your body is not attacking you, a virus is, a lightbulb turned on and has never gone out. I knew in my bones the information was true. I knew my body loves me and cares for me without conditions. And yours does too.

"I chose to suspend my disbelief and judgment and give it a try."

- Shannon Hake

CHAPTER 3

A VIRUS?

The question was, what virus could be attacking my body? The answer turned out to be the Epstein-Barr Virus (EBV). I was shocked and disbelieved. "I don't have a virus," I thought. Yet the more I read about the virus-caused symptoms, the more I understood that I do have a virus and more than one. I have had EBV living in my body since I was a little girl, and likely since I was an infant. I am betting the same is true for you, dear reader. The symptoms it has caused in my body are undeniable. Reading further, I learned EBV has mutated into over sixty varieties since it first appeared on the scene. An aggressive variety is the cause of MS.

    I found something in the book I could do to start killing off the EBV living in my body, the "Medical Medium 28-Day Healing Cleanse"[5]. I thought I would be healed after the cleanse was complete. Nope, I was wrong. I had my idea about the healing process and how long it should take. After all, my frame of reference was this: You get sick, go to the doctor, take antibiotics, and feel better in a week. But that's not how true healing works. That's how acute symptoms disappear, not long-term chronic symptoms. The cause of your sickness is still in your body, held at bay by your immune system, which is constantly fighting for you.

    Later, while re-reading about the cleanse, I found key points I missed, such as drinking at least a liter of water throughout the day. I still received unintended benefits; I lost 20 lbs, my warts started getting smaller or disappearing, and dry pre-cancerous spots on my face vanished. I completed the Cleanse while friends and family laughed and rolled their eyes. Maybe they thought it was like any other "health hack" or diet I had tried, and soon would return to eating as I had before.

After 28 days, I was disappointed that I wasn't healed, so I returned to eating 80% as I had before. The other 20%, I applied healing information as best I could. I guess what I was doing was "dabbling." I was not fully committed to giving it a chance. I continued dabbling for four years until I was getting worse and was completely frustrated. I had gained back the weight I lost and hadn't reversed any symptoms.

At this point, I was reduced to doing one "big" thing each day. A shower was a big thing. Weeding for 5 minutes in my garden was a big thing. Feeding the cat was a big thing. I also napped three times a day. My life and my brain were being whittled down to nothingness.

Once again, I was desperate for any relief. I scrolled through the book again, this time looking more closely at the protocols for different conditions & symptoms. The common denominator was celery juice. I started putting the pieces together and realized it was something important that I was missing. It was also one thing I hadn't tried.

But seriously, celery juice? "I'm not going to do that," I thought. However, the longer I thought about it, the more I realized that what I was doing had not helped my MS improve on any level. What was I so afraid of? Why was I so resistant? I tried so many other things, why not try this? When I finally made up my mind to try it, I kept reminding myself, "What do I have to lose, my illness?" And that is exactly what has been happening. The naysayers had nothing to lose, no incurable disease to battle, so it scared them. On the other hand, I had an entire life I wanted to live and felt like I was losing my battle. My quality of life was diminishing, and I was tired of being sick. So, without getting anyone's approval (I knew I would not get it anyway), I jumped in with both feet. I took a leap of faith and put a masticating celery juicer[3] on a payment plan. I was skeptical and disbelieved it could do anything for my MS, but I chose to suspend my disbelief and judgment and try it.

"I couldn't think of anything more important to spend my time doing than healing my body."

-Shannon Hake

CHAPTER 4

WHERE I STARTED

After the celery juicer arrived, I had no idea what I was doing, but I put into place what I had learned so far. Celery, preferably organic, needs rinsing and the ends cut off about ¼-½ inch before juicing. After juicing, it should be strained. It needs to be drunk on an empty stomach without anything added. It should also be 16 oz or more to start doing its job. I could start with as little as 1 oz and work my way up. I needed to wait 15 minutes to half an hour before eating or drinking anything else. Also, it's herbal medicine, not food. (Yes, celery is an herb.) That's all I knew at the time. But I started anyway and learned more as I went along.

    It wasn't until March 7, 2020, that I fully committed to juicing celery every day. It was a huge challenge for me. I struggled to have enough energy to stand and wash the celery and then stand to juice it. Cleaning the machine was an all-day task. I would clean a little, rest for a while, clean a little more, then take a nap. While not napping, I spent 80% of my day in the kitchen. Yet, I couldn't think of anything more important to spend my time doing than healing my body.

    So, what changes did I experience? At the end of the first week, I noticed that I had more energy throughout the day. At the end of the first month, I was napping only once a day. At the end of month 4, I didn't nap at all and had NO leg spasms at night. (I had them for 15 years) By the end of month six, I was not as affected by heat, cold water on my skin didn't feel like fire, and my brain fog[61] was lessening. I kept going, and by the end of the first year, I was hardly dizzy anymore (I had been dizzy for 5 years), and my seasonal allergies were completely gone. My body was starting to heal itself, one day at a time, *one millimeter* at a time.

During this time, I bought another book in the series, *Medical Medium Celery Juice, The Most Powerful Medicine of Our Time, Healing Millions Worldwide*[11]. In it, I read more details about the healing benefits of celery juice, what it does, and why it is so important. Since I had continuous, remarkable results, I trusted the information from Anthony William, the Medical Medium. He is also the source of celery juicing.

"I stopped eating foods...that feed pathogens, causing symptoms."

-Shannon Hake

CHAPTER 5

SIMPLE, NOT EASY

Healing MS is simple, but not easy. This is what I did. I juiced celery first thing in the morning, then waited 30 minutes before eating or drinking anything else. As my symptoms started to improve, I stopped eating Troublemaker Foods as best I could. These are foods that feed pathogens, causing symptoms. The pathogens eat and then eliminate their waste. This waste inflames our nerves, causing symptoms. When I did not notice major improvements, I read more in the first book, *Medical Medium, Secrets Behind Chronic and Mystery Illness and How to Finally Heal*[1]. I also listened to Medical Medium podcasts[29], watched Medical Medium YouTube videos[23], and bought four more books, *Medical Medium Liver Rescue*[16], *Medical Medium Thyroid Healing*[17], *Medical Medium Cleanse to Heal*[18], and *Medical Medium Life-Changing Foods*[19]. All of these books have healing information you can't find elsewhere. It is far above what medical research and science have discovered to date. They also have secrets about health. For example, vinegar used topically is great for your skin. If taken internally, it's terrible for your teeth and bones. When I searched for the answers, he was talking and writing about, I could not find them anywhere else.

   The information is so comprehensive that I could only read a little at a time. I found information about symptoms I wanted to heal and focused on them. I learned that I was not drinking the recommended lemon water every morning. I switched up my routine and started squeezing half a lemon into 16 oz of water. I would drink it first after I woke up, so it would flush my liver of the garbage it collected overnight. I would wait 30 minutes and then drink my freshly made celery juice. I would wait another 30 minutes and start my breakfast, an all-fruit smoothie - The Heavy Metal Detox Smoothie (HMDS[45]).

I had to adjust my mindset since my eating habits were unaccustomed to this routine. It took me a while to get my head around making a smoothie without yogurt. My mind thought I needed more than this to get me through the morning. My mind was wrong. I would eat more fruit when I became hungry. I learned that as my body was cleansing and healing itself, eating any fat (protein) before the evening would give me a liver/stomachache. It also prohibited my cleansing process.

A month after adding lemon water, I also started incorporating supplements to take me to the next level of healing. Unknowingly, I started off doing it wrong. I hadn't read the chapter in Cleanse to Heal, "What You Need to Know about Supplements."[21] So, I bought inexpensive supplements filled with things that were bad[47]. After months had passed, and noticing no further healing results, I dug deeper. I discovered MedicalMedium.com, a resource where I could find correct information while away from my books. This is also where I found the preferred supplements[48] and foods directory[49]. It had the correct clean supplements to buy and consume. When I started using these, I finally started seeing more results, such as migraines lessening in quantity each week. Yes, I had multiple every week. I did this for about a year and a half before I needed to up my game again. I started to remove food from Level 1. This included eggs, dairy (milk, cheese, butter, ghee, yogurt, cream, and kefir), gluten, soft drinks, and being mindful of salt consumption[14]. I again hit a plateau and did not see the results I wanted. I gradually removed things listed in Levels 2, 3, 4, and 5[31]. I did this over the following year.

Meanwhile, I continued removing bonus troublemakers[58], such as natural/artificial flavors, nutritional yeast, citric acid, fats (proteins), salt, and alcohol. I also continued adding the three C's: Clean, Critical, Carbohydrates[56] (honey, fruit, steamed potatoes, sweet potatoes, coconut water, and winter squash), and Healing foods, such as parsley, cilantro, kale, dandelion greens, oranges, bananas, brussel sprouts, asparagus, and wild blueberries, to name just a few. The recipes in all the Medical Medium books kept me moving forward. I learned about Brain cell foods, Filler foods, and Brain betrayer Foods[50], as well as new ways to prepare them and keep my body healing.

When I had a handle on which foods to eat more and which to avoid, I started the Simplified 3:6:9 Cleanse[30]. This nine-day cleanse gently uproots pathogens and toxins[30]. It cleans your liver of unwanted things it has held inside to protect you, and works at 70% of the Original 3:6:9 Cleanse.[62] It was a great cleanse for me as a beginner. Three months later, I did the Original 3:6:9 Cleanse[32]. Its purpose is to uproot deep-seated toxins and pathogens[32].

To this day, I follow the Original 3:6:9 Cleanse[62] every 2-3 months[57].

"Once you know the truth, you can't un-know it."

-Shannon Hake

"This has never been about eating for my palate. It's been about eating foods that will help heal my MS."

-Shannon Hake

CHAPTER 6

KNOW YOUR WHY

When you have an invisible condition like multiple sclerosis, others without it have a tough time understanding what you are going through. They have a harder time understanding when you go against what doctors say will slow its progression. However, once you know the truth, you can't un-know it. If you know what's wrong, you've taken the first step toward healing. My body was completely aligned with the truth, and it was healing.

As I kept going day after day, my family struggled with my new way of eating. They didn't understand why I wouldn't eat cheese or eggs anymore. This was the hardest part for me emotionally. It's hard enough to be sick, but to feel you have no family and few friends on your side to support you is brutal. I had to firmly know why I was eating what I was eating and why I wasn't eating other things.

This has never been about eating for my palate. It's been about eating foods that will help heal my MS and its accompanying symptoms. The crazy thing is that I enjoy eating the healing foods more than I ever enjoyed eating the troublemaker foods. Troublemaker foods feed the pathogens living inside my body. I took away their food and fed myself food they wouldn't eat. What we eat matters more than what we've been taught.

I started craving healing foods I couldn't tolerate before, such as oranges and brussel sprouts. I started thoroughly enjoying the simplicity of my meals and snacks. A red apple has become my daily afternoon snack. Sometimes I add a date and celery sticks. My lunches and dinners are a giant salad with various greens, fresh herbs, and steamed potatoes or sweet potatoes. I have more energy every day; It's more than I've had in 30 years.

My "why" was that I was eliminating the cause of my MS. Yet could it be as simple as not feeding the pathogens? Not completely. I needed to start repairing and rebuilding the damage they had caused. This is where the right supplements helped take me to the next level of healing.

Cat's claw, lemon balm, B12 (as Adenosylcobalamin and Methylcobalamin), Zinc (as Zinc Sulfate), ALA, melatonin, and vitamin C (as Micro C) are supplements I take regularly. Cat's Claw is essential for destroying viruses, bacteria, and other unfriendly microorganisms. These can hang out inside the liver. "Cat's claw is an herbal medicine... which is used for its antiinflammatory "[sic]" and immune modulating "[sic]" effects in the treatment of fever, fatigue, muscle and joint aches and the symptoms of chronic inflammatory conditions"[33] such as Multiple Sclerosis.

Lemon balm does the same thing. It calms nerves inside the lining of the intestines. This, in turn, lowers damaging heat inside the liver. Lemon balm supports the adrenals and "helps with sleep"[34].

Vitamin C helps with white blood cell recuperation and recovery from fighting viruses and bacteria. It also impairs pathogens exposed to it. "Important functions of the body, such as immune response, pulmonary function, and iron absorption are related to vitamin C intakes"[35]

ALA (Alpha Lipoic Acid) helps repair the myelin nerve sheath. It also helps repair damaged neurons and neurotransmitters. A Neurochemical Research article says, "α-LA produces its neuroprotective effect by inhibiting reactive oxygen species formation and neuronal damage, modulating protein levels, and promoting neurotransmitters and antioxidant levels."[40]

Melatonin helps repair and grow neurons. It also reduces inflammation in the brain. One medical research study noted, "Melatonin promotes adaptation through allostasis and stands out as an endogenous, dietary, and therapeutic molecule with important health benefits"[39]

"Brain cell foods nourish our bodies and don't feed pathogens."

- Shannon Hake

CHAPTER 7

KNOW BETTER, DO BETTER

About three years into my healing process, I told my daughter I noticed she was doing something so kind. She quoted Maya Angelou, "When you know better, you do better." Yes, doing better is what I've been doing the whole time. My body didn't have a choice. I had to push through the abundance of misinformation that healthcare providers unknowingly gave me. It's not their fault. It's what they were taught in medical school and continuing education.

Knowing what I know now, I do better. I know there is a difference between brain cell foods, filler foods, and brain betrayer foods[60]. Brain cell foods[59] nourish our bodies and don't feed pathogens. Filler foods don't nourish our bodies, yet they don't feed pathogens. Brain betrayer foods feed pathogens, making it easier for them to proliferate, cause inflammation, and create symptoms.

I choose to do better whenever I put anything into my mouth. This is true for the liquids I drink, the desserts I eat, and everything in between. I no longer live in fear of what symptoms might randomly show up. I live in confidence that they won't. And *if* a symptom appears, I know what to do about it. Having peace in health is priceless.

"My body is made to heal, and it will."

-Shannon Hake

CHAPTER 8

HOW DO YOU HEAL?

The most important part of healing is knowing your body *can* heal. The second most important part is knowing what to do. When I shifted my mind from "my body is confused and is attacking itself" to "my body is made to heal, and it will," I relaxed. I was empowered, solid, and excited to start. Our bodies are designed to heal themselves. Our bodies are miraculous. After all, who still has a scrape on their knee from when they were a child? Or a broken bone from falling off a skateboard?

How do you heal a chronic illness such as MS? The goal is to starve the pathogens causing the disease and then repair and rebuild the damage they have caused. It really is that simple, but it's not easy. Think of the labyrinth game where you move the ball from one end of the board to the other while avoiding the holes. It's like that. It's a simple game, but it's not easy. The healing and filler foods are the track. The troublemaker foods are the holes.

Remember the various levels of food I removed over time? Pathogens love to eat those foods. After eating, they excrete, our nerves become inflamed, and we get symptoms. We may not get symptoms right away. We might get symptoms in a week or two, a month, or a year later. Everyone's nerves have a different tolerance. But once the tolerance is reached, symptoms don't easily disappear. The same applies to healing. Everyone's body heals on its own schedule, so you cannot judge yourself. It's not a linear process. It takes time and patience. Boy, does it take patience! It takes awareness. It takes loving yourself enough to go against the grain; to have faith and take the path that guides you to health.

The beautiful part of healing is that you get to choose what's right for your body. If you understand why you are doing what you're doing, you'll keep going. You won't want to cheat because you'll understand the consequences of doing so.

THIS IS HOW I'VE BEEN HEALING MY MS:

When	What	Why
Morning, upon waking	Rinse mouth with warm water, then brush teeth	It kills and flushes bacteria, cleans teeth
After clearing the mouth of overnight bacterial growth	Drink 16-32 oz. lemon water, wait 30 minutes before eating or drinking anything else.	It flushes my liver of garbage collected overnight; a 30-minute wait gives it time to do its job.
30 minutes after drinking lemon water	Drink organic fresh celery juice, 32 oz. daily. When I began, I started at 2 oz. and moved up from there. Ideally, you want	Kills bacteria and viruses, restores bile, strengthens Hydrochloric acid in the gut, feeds every cell in the endocrine system, removes toxic salts from the liver, feeds

When	What	Why
	16 oz.- 32 oz. daily.	good gut bacteria and more.
30 minutes after drinking celery juice	Drink MM Heavy Metal Detox Smoothie (HMDS)[45].	To remove heavy metals throughout my body over time.
When I get hungry before noon	Eat fresh fruit, drink freshly squeezed juice, and sip on lemon water.	To keep my body releasing toxins from eating foods grown with pesticides, fungicides, rodenticides, & herbicides. To keep my body hydrated with living fluids.
When I'm hungry at lunchtime or after	Eat food from any of the Medical Medium books. It's usually steamed potatoes/ sweet potatoes and a liver rescue salad. Sip on lemon water.	To keep my body fueled with easily assimilable phytonutrients that help rebuild and restore damaged parts and keep starving any pathogen. Stay hydrated.

When	What	Why
Afternoon snack	Red apple[51], with a Medjool date[52] and a celery stick[53], sip on lemon water.	To clean my colon, hydrate on a cellular level, expel mucus, and reduce inflammation.
Dinner time	Eat food from any of the Medical Medium books. Spinach soup is one of my favorites. I drink lemon water when I take my supplements.	To keep my body fueled with easily assimilable phytonutrients that help rebuild and restore damaged parts and keep starving any pathogen. Stay hydrated.
Evening	Drink herbal tea, eat a red apple, Clean, Critical, Carbohydrates (CCC[56]), or filler foods if still hungry. Drink the last of my 16-32 oz. lemon water.	To keep pathogen-fighting herbs in my bloodstream so any symptom I'm focused on can continue healing overnight.

Please Remember:

- I said it is Simple, But Not Easy
- The source of all healing information I used comes from the Medical Medium Book Series. Using other information could lead you down the wrong path. It's always your choice.
- It's important to READ his books, not just have them in your library
- It takes persistence, patience, and time
- You are worth the time it takes for YOUR body to heal itself
- You CAN do this if you truly want to heal
- It's never too late to begin
- If you "cheat", forgive yourself and do better next time
- KEEP GOING

"My body desperately wanted to heal. I searched high and low to find a way to heal. Once found, I never looked back."

-Shannon Hake

"I empowered myself to heal myself. No one knows your body better than you."

-Shannon Hake

CHAPTER 9

OTHER SYMPTOMS HEALED

These are symptoms unrelated to MS that have been healed.

Toenail fungus, acid reflux, seasonal allergies, chronic ear pain, sinus bleeding, varicose veins, improved eyesight, hot flashes, night sweats, heart palpitations, scoliosis, chronic back pain, liver spots, *tinnitus, and warts, *dry eyes.

MS symptoms healed:

Muscle spasms, heat sensitivities, fatigue, numbness, tingling, nystagmus, dizziness, brain fog[61], vision loss, skin sensitivities, difficulty staying awake, difficulty staying asleep, *trouble walking, balance issues, muscle cramps, vertigo, difficulty thinking, heavy legs, left-side weakness, *drop foot, inability to rapidly change motions, peristaltic action/constipation, depression, *bladder leakage, excessive urination at night, stiff muscles, *headaches, *bladder urgency, *bladder frequency, *migraines, *overactive reflexes.

*Improved and still healing completely

"When you have neurological symptoms or a condition with an unknown cause, it takes time to heal. There is no 'cure.' You must heal yourself. Your nervous system has been under attack. It takes time to heal your nerves after killing the pathogens. Be patient and persistent. You can do it."

    -Shannon Hake

"You can't argue with success."

    -Carolyn Ansted

FAQ

- What amount of celery juice do you drink?

I started with 2 oz. and worked my way up to 16 oz. Now I drink 32 oz every morning.

- What number of stalks makes 32 oz?

2-3 bunches, depending on size and stalk hydration.

- How do you know what supplements to take and what dosage?

There are protocols for hundreds of symptoms and conditions in almost every book in the series.

- What is HMDS?

Heavy Metal Detox Smoothie (recipe[45])

- Can I get all the detox ingredients in my body without eating an HMDS?

Yes. You can eat the five key ingredients separately within 24 hours and still receive help from the HMDS.

- What are the five key ingredients in the HMDS?

1. Cilantro 2. Barley Grass Juice Extract Powder 3. Spirulina 4. Atlantic Dulse 5. Wild Blueberries

- Where do you get the ingredients?

I go to the supplement directory at MedicalMedium.com. 75% of my supplements are from vimergy.com. I get other suggested supplements from grocery stores, health food stores, and Amazon.

- Do you ever get tired of drinking celery juice?
No. Do you ever get tired of feeling better and better?

- Are your lesions gone?
No. Lesions are not the cause of MS symptoms; neurotoxins from viruses are.

- How do you know when you are healed?
When you feel better and your symptoms are gone. Stay on the path. It happens over time.

- Why celery juice?
Because celery juice is an herb that kills viruses, bacteria, and other bad microbes, it restores the seven-acid blend of HCL in the gut. It strengthens your bile. It is the ultimate neurotransmitter chemical. It rejuvenates the liver overall. It is a complete electrolyte. See more in the book Medical Medium Celery Juice[11].

- Can I add anything to the celery juice?
No. This removes any benefits it offers.

- Do I have to eat this way for the rest of my life?
No. You can eat how you want. It's always your choice. If you still have symptoms, you are feeding pathogens, have heavy metals, or other toxins in your body. It's best to starve the pathogens and remove heavy metals and other toxins.

- Why do you strain the celery after juicing it?
Little particles left over can obstruct the pure, unimpeded juice from doing its healing work.

- Why do you rely solely on Medical Medium information, not doctors' information?

I have used doctors' information with no lasting results. Medical Medium information has given me continuous results for over 6 years.

- Where do you get your wild blueberries?

I find them in my local grocery store. I use Wyman's wild blueberries, frozen in a 3 lb. bag.

- Why do you drink HMDS every day?

Heavy metals settle in the body, anywhere. To remove them, one needs to pull them out consistently. This happens over time, not just once.

- Why do you put freshly squeezed lemon juice in your water?

Lemon juice has healing power. When put in water, it brings the water alive.

- Why do you use room temperature water in your lemon water?

Using hot water destroys the most important aspect of what lemon juice can do for you[55]. In tea, hot water is fine to use, not in your lemon water.

- Why do you drink 16-32 oz. lemon water first thing every morning after rinsing your mouth with warm water?

My liver needs enough water to stay hydrated and flush the garbage collected overnight. My mouth needs flushing to get rid of bacteria collected overnight.

- Can I use ready-made lemon juice that I find in the grocery store or lemon essential oil?

No. Ready-made lemon juice includes things you don't want to consume. Lemon essential oil is different than lemon juice and will not do the same thing.[55] If it were me, I would not take essential oils internally.

- What are Healing, Filler, and Troublemaker foods?

Healing foods nourish your body and starve pathogens: fruits, vegetables, herbs, spices, wild foods. Filler foods will not feed pathogens, yet they won't give your body critical nutrients either. Harmful foods feed pathogens that cause symptoms.

- What are Clean, Critical, Carbohydrates?

"Healthy carbohydrates that provide our organs, tissues, muscles, and cells with the glucose they need to help us stay alive and thrive"[56].

°Fruit °Raw Honey °Potatoes and sweet potatoes °Winter squash °Coconut water

TIPS

- Lemon water: use lukewarm or cooler temperature water, never hot
- Apples: choose red ones
- Eating mistake: Forgive yourself and consciously choose to do better for your next bite
- Eating: Remember you are starving pathogens, not your body
- Diet: Choose one you can sustain
- Bananas: Do not eat unripe or overly ripe ones. They are ripe when they are mostly yellow with small brown spots. Over time, you will learn to gauge when they are perfectly ripe.
- Fats: If eating fats, save them until noon or after, preferably until dinnertime
- Hydration: Drink living water throughout the day- coconut water (with nothing added) or ½ a lemon squeezed in filtered water
- HMDS: You can use a whole orange instead of juicing an orange for the HMDS.
- Cooked Food: Cooked foods are dehydrating. Eat colorful raw foods as often as you can.
- Liver: Remember, your liver is your garbage collector. Clean it as often as possible with the 3:6:9 Cleanse.
- Lymphatic system: Your lymphatic system is just an overflow for your liver. Focus on your liver health, and lymph health will follow.

- Notes: Keep notes on your progress. When looking back, it is amazing to see how far you have come.
- Protein: Protein = Fat (think nuts, seeds, meat, cheese, milk, nut butters. All are fatty)
- Fats: When healing, lower your fat/protein intake
- Medicine: Remember, celery juice is a medicine, not a caloric food
- Protein: Small amounts of highly bioavailable and bioassimilable protein exist in every fruit and vegetable. You don't ever have to worry about getting enough. We do not need as much as they say.
- Overweight: If you are overweight, you most likely have a liver issue. If you have never cleaned out your filter (liver), it's time for a Medical Medium 3:6:9 cleanse from *Cleanse to Heal*[18].
- Fruit of any kind: Eat fruit before you eat anything fatty. Fruit digests quickly and will hinder fat digestion.

ABOUT THE AUTHOR

Shannon Hake was diagnosed with Relapsing/Remitting Multiple Sclerosis (RRMS) in 2001. She took medications, had relapses, and used walking aids. In 2015, she was given the book *Medical Medium: Secrets Behind Chronic and Mystery Illness and How to Finally Heal*. After dabbling with the information for 5 years, in March 2020, she took her health into her own hands and fully committed. She not only has been healing her MS but has also been healing other unrelated symptoms.

When I met Shannon, we were sitting next to each other at a fun healer's group. That was the beginning of a 14-year-long friendship in which I have seen her help so many, including myself. I have seen her smile through incredible pain...both physically and emotionally...Not because she is weak, but because she is strong.

Shannon is not a scientist nor a magician. She is a Songbird. That is what I call her, anyhow. You see, a Songbird is who we hear as the raging storm subsides, and reminds us that all storms end. To stand against the storm of disbelief takes courage. It takes the inner ability to listen to the instinctual guidance and song within, rather than the words of another. Many times, Shannon has not only offered this song to me while I was in my own raging storms but also reminded me that I, too, have a song. I know she will do the same for you.

Keep singing, Songbird!

    -- Deb Yeats, extraordinary healer and friend

REFERENCES, SOURCES, CITATIONS

1. William, Anthony. *Medical Medium, Secrets Behind Chronic and Mystery Illness and How to Finally Heal*, Hay House, 2015.

2. William, Anthony. *Revised & Expanded, Medical Medium, Secrets Behind Chronic and Mystery Illness and How to Finally Heal*, Hay House, 2021, p. 276.

3. William, Anthony. *Medical Medium, Celery Juice, The Most Powerful Medicine of our Time, Healing Millions Worldwide*, Hay House, 2019, p. 94.

4. William, Anthony. *Medical Medium, Thyroid Healing, The Truth Behind Hashimoto's, Graves', Insomnia, Hypothyroidism, Thyroid Nodules & Epstein-Barr*, Hay House, 2017, p. 139.

5. William, Anthony. *Revised & Expanded, Medical Medium, Secrets Behind Chronic and Mystery Illness and How to Finally Heal*, Hay House, 2021, pp 280-291.

6. Ibid., p. 71.

7. William, Anthony. *Medical Medium, Thyroid Healing, The Truth Behind Hashimoto's, Graves', Insomnia, Hypothyroidism, Thyroid Nodules & Epstein-Barr*, Hay House, 2017, p. 128.

8. William, Anthony. *Medical Medium, Brain Saver, Answers to Brain Inflammation, Mental Health, OCD, Brain Fog, Neurological Symptoms, Addiction, Anxiety, Depression, Heavy Metals, Epstein Barr Virus, Seizures, Lyme, ADHD, Alzheimer's, Autoimmune & Eating Disorders*, Hay House, 2022, p. 531.

9. Ibid., p. 528.

10. William, Anthony. *Medical Medium, Thyroid Healing, The Truth Behind Hashimoto's, Graves', Insomnia, Hypothyroidism, Thyroid Nodules & Epstein-Barr*, Hay House, 2017, p. xix.

11. William, Anthony. *Medical Medium Celery Juice, The Most Powerful Medicine of Our Time, Healing Millions Worldwide*, Hay House, 2019.

12. William, Anthony. *Medical Medium, Thyroid Healing, The Truth Behind Hashimoto's, Graves', Insomnia, Hypothyroidism, Thyroid Nodules & Epstein-Barr*, Hay House, 2017, p. 5.

13. William, Anthony. *Medical Medium Celery Juice, The Most Powerful Medicine of Our Time, Healing Millions Worldwide*, Hay House, 2019, p. 25.

14. William, Anthony. *Revised & Expanded, Medical Medium, Secrets Behind Chronic and Mystery Illness and How to Finally Heal*, Hay House, 2021, p. 250.

15. Ibid., p. 261.

16. William, Anthony. *Medical Medium Liver Rescue, Answers to Eczema, Psoriasis, Diabetes, Strep, Acne, Gout, Bloating, Gallstones, Adrenal Stress, Fatigue, Fatty Liver, Weight Issues, SIBO & Autoimmune Disease*, Hay House, 2018.

17. William, Anthony. *Medical Medium, Thyroid Healing, The Truth Behind Hashimoto's, Graves', Insomnia, Hypothyroidism, Thyroid Nodules & Epstein-Barr*, Hay House, 2017.

18. William, Anthony. *Medical Medium Cleanse to Heal, Healing Plans for Sufferers of Anxiety, Depression, Acne, Eczema, Lyme, Gut Problems, Brain Fog, Weight Issues, Migraines, Bloating, Vertigo, Psoriasis, Cysts, Fatigue, PCOS, Fibroids, UTI, Endometriosis & Autoimmune*, Hay House, 2020.

19. William, Anthony. *Medical Medium, Life-Changing Foods, Save Yourself and the Ones You Love with the Hidden Powers of Fruits & Vegetables*, Hay House, 2016.

20. William, Anthony. *Medical Medium Cleanse to Heal, Healing Plans for Sufferers of Anxiety, Depression, Acne, Eczema, Lyme, Gut Problems, Brain Fog, Weight Issues, Migraines, Bloating, Vertigo, Psoriasis, Cysts, Fatigue, PCOS, Fibroids, UTI, Endometriosis & Autoimmune*, Hay House, 2020, p. 478.

21. Ibid., p. 472.

22. William, Anthony, host. "Kidney Health – Radio Show Archive." Medical Medium Podcast, Spotify app, 28 Aug. 2017.

23. William, Anthony, host. "Health Symptoms & Conditions Q & A – Exercising & Rebounding with Chronic Illness." YouTube VIDEO, 30 Sept. 2023.

24. William, Anthony. *Medical Medium, Thyroid Healing, The Truth Behind Hashimoto's, Graves', Insomnia, Hypothyroidism, Thyroid Nodules & Epstein-Barr*, Hay House, 2017, p.104.

25. William, Anthony. *Medical Medium Liver Rescue, Answers to Eczema, Psoriasis, Diabetes, Strep, Acne, Gout, Bloating, Gallstones, Adrenal Stress, Fatigue, Fatty Liver, Weight Issues, SIBO & Autoimmune Disease*, Hay House, 2018, p. 301.

26. Ibid., p. 303.

27. William, Anthony, host. "Foods That Heal Chronic Illness – Radio Show Archive." Medical Medium Podcast, Spotify app, 31 Oct. 2016.

28. William, Anthony. *Medical Medium Celery Juice, The Most Powerful Medicine of Our Time, Healing Millions Worldwide*, Hay House, 2019, p. 31.

29. William, Anthony, host. "Truth About Multiple Sclerosis – Radio Show Archive." Medical Medium Podcast, Soundcloud app, 16 Mar. 2017.

30. William, Anthony. *Medical Medium Cleanse to Heal, Healing Plans for Sufferers of Anxiety, Depression, Acne, Eczema, Lyme, Gut Problems, Brain Fog, Weight Issues, Migraines, Bloating, Vertigo, Psoriasis, Cysts, Fatigue, PCOS, Fibroids, UTI, Endometriosis & Autoimmune*, Hay House, 2020, p. 130.

31. William, Anthony. *Revised & Expanded, Medical Medium, Secrets Behind Chronic and Mystery Illness and How to Finally Heal*, Hay House, 2021, pp. 250-258.

32. William, Anthony. *Medical Medium Cleanse to Heal, Healing Plans for Sufferers of Anxiety, Depression, Acne, Eczema, Lyme, Gut Problems, Brain Fog, Weight Issues, Migraines, Bloating, Vertigo, Psoriasis, Cysts, Fatigue, PCOS, Fibroids, UTI, Endometriosis & Autoimmune*, Hay House, 2020, p. 109.

33. "Cat's Claw." PubMed, 2012, pubmed.ncbi.nlm.nih.gov/31643645.

34. Safari, Mostafa, et al. "The Effects of Melissa Officinalis on Depression and Anxiety in Type 2 Diabetes Patients With Depression: A Randomized Double-blinded Placebo-controlled Clinical Trial." BMC Complementary Medicine and Therapies, vol. 23, no. 1, May 2023, https://doi.org/10.1186/s12906-023-03978-x.

35. "Vitamin C and Human Health--a Review of Recent Data Relevant to Human Requirements." PubMed, 1996, pubmed.ncbi.nlm.nih.gov/8698541.

36. William, Anthony. *Medical Medium Liver Rescue, Answers to Eczema, Psoriasis, Diabetes, Strep, Acne, Gout, Bloating, Gallstones, Adrenal Stress, Fatigue, Fatty Liver, Weight Issues, SIBO & Autoimmune Disease*, Hay House, 2018, p. 307.

37. William, Anthony. *Medical Medium, Secrets Behind Chronic and Mystery Illness and How to Finally Heal,* Hay House, 2015, p. 160.

38. Ibid., p. 67.

39. Chitimus, Diana Maria, et al. "Melatonin's Impact on Antioxidative and Anti-Inflammatory Reprogramming in Homeostasis and Disease." Biomolecules, vol. 10, no. 9, Aug. 2020, p. 1211. https://doi.org/10.3390/biom10091211.

40. Khan, H., Singh, T.G., Dahiya, R.S. et al. α-Lipoic Acid, an Organosulfur Biomolecule a Novel Therapeutic Agent for Neurodegenerative Disorders: An Mechanistic Perspective. Neurochem Res 47, 1853–1864 (2022). https://doi.org/10.1007/s11064-022-03598-w.

41. William, Anthony. *Medical Medium, Life-Changing Foods, Save Yourself and the Ones You Love with the Hidden Powers of Fruits & Vegetables*, Hay House, 2016, p. 23.

42. Frost, Robert. "The Road Not Taken." The Poetry Foundation, 12 Aug. 2024, www.poetryfoundation.org/poems/44272/the-road-not-taken.

43. William, Anthony, host. "Rising Out Of The Ashes – Radio Show Archive." Medical Medium Podcast, Soundcloud app, 18 Oct. 2016.

44. William, Anthony [Medical Medium]. "Your God Given Right To Heal". Medical Medium Message, Telegram app, 8 Oct. 2024.

45. William, Anthony. *Medical Medium, Brain Saver Protocols, Cleanses & Recipes, For Neurological, Autoimmune & Mental Health*, Hay House, 2022, p. 264.

46. William, Anthony [Medical Medium]. "Our Bodies Want To Heal". Medical Medium Message, Telegram app, 13 Sept. 2023.

47. William, Anthony. "Are Supplements Necessary?" https://www.medicalmedium.com/blog/are-supplements-necessary. 11-Jan-2017.

48. William, Anthony. https://www.medicalmedium.com/preferred/supplements.

49. William, Anthony. https://www.medicalmedium.com/preferred/food.

50. William, Anthony. *Medical Medium, Brain Saver, Answers to Brain Inflammation, Mental Health, OCD, Brain Fog, Neurological Symptoms, Addiction, Anxiety, Depression, Heavy Metals, Epstein-Barr Virus, Seizures, Lyme, ADHD, Alzheimer's, Autoimmune & Eating Disorders*, Hay House, 2022, p. 437.

51. William, Anthony. https://www.medicalmedium.com/blog/apples-colon-cleanser.

52. William, Anthony. https://www.medicalmedium.com/blog/apple-cinnamon-stuffed-dates.

53. William, Anthony. https://www.medicalmedium.com/blog/celery.

54. William, Anthony, host. "075 Your God Given Right To Heal: Deep Wisdom & Truths To Help You On The Healing Path." Medical Medium Podcast, SoundCloud app, 7 Dec. 2024.

55. William, Anthony, host. "020 Lemon Water: Is It Really That Bad?" Medical Medium Podcast, Spotify app, https://open.spotify.com/episode/2bdjuK4uDRmySOEximagZo?si=g3mqPMICQ_-NG965slSdDg, 5 July 2022.

56. William, Anthony. https://www.medicalmedium.com/blog/critical-clean-carbohydrates.

57. William, Anthony. https://www.medicalmedium.com/blog/the-options-are-delightful-and-delicious

58. William, Anthony. https://www.medicalmedium.com/blog/troublemakers-that-make-us-sick-food-chemicals.

www.ingramcontent.com/pod-product-compliance
Lightning Source LLC
Chambersburg PA
CBHW022125040426
42450CB00006B/859